MCR

NOV 0 8 2010

WEATHERWISE

GASES, PRESSURE, and WIND

| The Science of the **ATMOSPHERE** |

Paul Fleisher

LERNER PUBLICATIONS COMPANY · MINNEAPOLIS

Lerner Publications Company
A division of Lerner Publishing Group, Inc.
241 First Avenue North
Minneapolis, MN 55401 U.S.A.

Website address: www.lernerbooks.com

Library of Congress Cataloging-in-Publication Data

Fleisher, Paul.
    Gases, pressure, and wind : the science of the atmosphere /
by Paul Fleisher.
       p.   cm. — (Weatherwise)
    Includes bibliographical references and index.
    ISBN 978–0–8225–7537–5 (lib. bdg. : alk. paper)
    1. Atmospheric physics—Juvenile literature. 2. Meteorology—
Juvenile literature. I. Title.
QC863.5.F54 2011
551.5—dc22   2009044916

Manufactured in the United States of America
1 – PC – 7/15/10

CONTENTS

| INTRODUCTION |

"What's the weather like today?" That's one of the first questions many of us ask each morning. Is it cloudy or sunny? Warm or cold? Is it going to rain?

Weather affects how we spend each day. Weather affects our comfort and safety. It affects how our food grows. But what is weather? And why is it always changing?

Most simply, weather is what's happening in the air around us. Earth is wrapped in a blanket of air called the atmosphere. The atmosphere is constantly moving and changing. So the weather is always changing too.

The study of weather is called meteorology. Weather scientists, or meteorologists, study how weather changes from day to day and from minute to minute. They also study weather patterns. They measure temperatures and winds. They record rainfall and snowfall. The patterns that meteorologists find help predict what weather may be coming next.

FASCINATING FACT:

In ancient Greece, the philosopher Aristotle wrote a book about weather. His book was called *Meteorologica*. It was written in about 340 B.C.

A STATUE OF THE PHILOSOPHER ARISTOTLE, AUTHOR OF *METEOROLOGICA*

WEATHER AND CLIMATE

What's the difference between weather and climate? Weather is the state of the atmosphere in a certain place at any one time. Climate is the typical weather of a place.

Climate describes weather averages and extremes. Some places have a rainy climate. Some places have a cold climate. Some places have a warm and dry climate. We can't predict the weather for a certain day by knowing the climate. But we can know what kind of weather is most likely.

CHAPTER ONE

EARTH'S ATMOSPHERE

The atmosphere contains all the air we need to live on Earth. But compared to the size of Earth as a whole, the atmosphere is very thin. It reaches only about 60 miles (100 kilometers) above the ground. That may sound high. But suppose you used an apple to represent Earth. The atmosphere would be thinner than the apple's skin.

The atmosphere has several layers. The lowest layer is the troposphere. Air conditions are always changing in the troposphere. All weather takes place in this layer. On average, the troposphere is about 6.6 miles (11 km) thick. It's thicker—about 10 miles (16 km) deep—near the equator (the imaginary line that runs around the center of Earth). At the poles, it's thinner—only about 3.6 miles (6 km) deep.

The higher you go, the less dense the air becomes. This means gas molecules such as oxygen in the air are spaced farther apart. (A molecule is the smallest part of a substance that has all the properties of that substance. Air is made up of molecules of different gases.) Temperatures get colder at higher altitudes (heights) too. At the top of the troposphere, the air is about −75°F (−60°C).

Above the troposphere is the stratosphere. It reaches up to about 30 miles (50 km) above Earth. Air conditions in this layer don't change much from day to day.

Most airplanes fly in the troposphere.

The stratosphere contains small amounts of the gas ozone. Ozone is a special form of oxygen. It absorbs harmful ultraviolet (UV) rays from the sun. UV rays cause sunburn. They can even be deadly. The ozone layer in the stratosphere protects life on Earth.

Above the stratosphere are two other layers. They are called the mesosphere and the thermosphere. The air in these layers is very thin. The gas molecules are spaced very far apart. Beyond these layers is the emptiness of space.

But we're interested in weather. So the troposphere is where everything is happening.

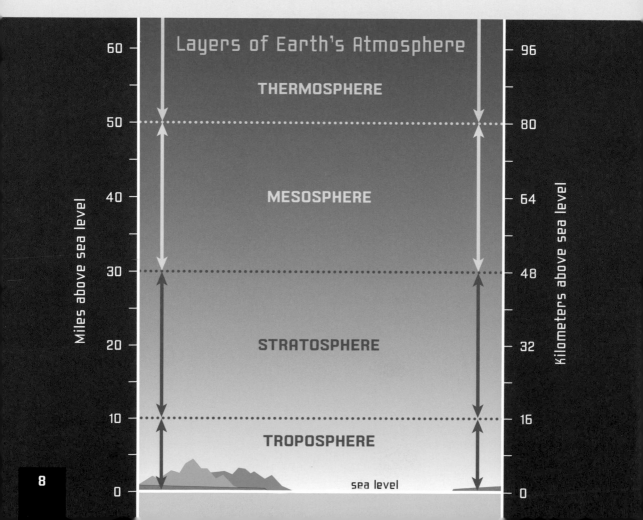

Layers of Earth's Atmosphere

THERMOSPHERE

MESOSPHERE

STRATOSPHERE

TROPOSPHERE

sea level

Miles above sea level

60
50
40
30
20
10
0

Kilometers above sea level

96
80
64
48
32
16
0

TRAINING AT ALTITUDE

Some athletes train in the mountains. The air is thinner at these heights. There is less oxygen to breathe. At first, it is hard for athletes to exercise with less oxygen. Over time, their bodies adjust to the thin air. They make more red blood cells, which move oxygen around the body. Their hearts get stronger and can pump more blood through their bodies. High-altitude training helps them perform better at lower altitudes, where there is once again more oxygen to breathe.

SOME RUNNERS MAKE SPECIAL TRIPS TO TRAIN AT HIGH ALTITUDES.

WHAT IS AIR?

Air is all around us. But it's easy to forget it's there. We can't see it. We usually can't smell it. We feel it only when the wind is blowing.

Air is a mixture of clear, colorless gases. About 78 percent—almost four-fifths—of dry air is nitrogen. About 21 percent, or just over one-fifth, is oxygen. Plants and animals need oxygen to live. About 1 percent of the air is made of other gases. Air also contains water vapor, or water in gas form.

About half the air in the atmosphere is found in the lowest 3.5 miles (5.5 km). Above that, the air is thin, making it hard to breathe. Just 1 mile (1.6 km) higher, there's not enough air for a person to live for more than a few hours.

Carbon dioxide makes up a very small part of the air. But it is an important part. Plants take in carbon dioxide. They use water, sunlight, and carbon dioxide to make food so they can grow. This food-making process is called photosynthesis.

Air also contains trillions of tiny particles called aerosols. Most are too small to see. Some are tiny grains of dust or sand. Others are tiny salt crystals from ocean spray. Some aerosols come from volcanoes. Aerosols come from forest fires, factory smoke, and car exhaust too. Aerosols play an important part in creating weather. Water vapor collects on these particles. The vapor turns into water droplets. They group together to form clouds and rain.

WHEN MANY AEROSOLS ARE PRESENT ON A STILL DAY, THEY ARE VISIBLE AS HAZE OR SMOG.

AIR PRESSURE

The force of gravity holds air close to Earth. Gravity keeps air from drifting away into space. It gives air weight. The air presses on Earth's surface and everything on it. This is called air pressure. We don't feel the air pressing on us. Our bodies are used to the pressure.

Air pressure is greatest near the ground. At higher altitudes, less air presses down from above. So air pressure decreases as we move higher in the atmosphere.

Meteorologists measure air pressure with a tool called a barometer. Air pressure is measured in millibars. At sea level, average air pressure is slightly more than 1,000 millibars. Denver, Colorado, is about 1 mile (1.6 km) high. Its air pressure is only about 850 millibars.

AIR IS REALLY THERE

We can't see it. But air is a substance. Here's how to prove it. You'll need a bowl and a clear drinking glass. Fill the bowl with water. Turn the glass upside down. Push it straight down into the water. Watch what happens.

The glass does not fill with water. Why not? Because it's already filled with something else—air. The air keeps water out of the glass.

THIS OLD-FASHIONED INSTRUMENT INCLUDES A THERMOMETER *(TOP)* AND A BAROMETER *(BOTTOM)*.

FASCINATING FACT:
INCHES OF MERCURY

The first barometer was an upside-down glass tube filled with liquid mercury. The mercury rose or fell in the tube as the air pressure changed. So barometric pressure is sometimes measured in inches of mercury—the inches it reached in the tube. The average air pressure at sea level is about 30 inches (76 cm) of mercury.

Pressure plays a big part in producing weather. Air expands (spreads out) when it is warm. There is less gas in the same space—less gas pressing down. So warm air has lower pressure than cold air. Warm air can also hold more water vapor, which is lighter than most gases in the air. So moist air has lower pressure than dry air. High pressure usually means cooler, drier air.

You often hear meteorologists talk about high and low pressure systems. They may just call them highs and lows. The cool, dry air in a high pressure system means the skies are clear. The weather is fair. Warm, moist air in a low pressure system brings clouds and rain. Storms form around areas of low pressure.

Air pressure differences also produce wind. High pressure always pushes air toward areas of lower pressure. So winds always blow from high pressure toward low pressure. The moving air carries weather conditions around the globe, keeping the atmosphere in constant motion.

CHAPTER TWO
WHAT DRIVES THE WEATHER?

Weather has amazing power. A tornado can rip buildings apart. A hurricane can destroy an entire city. Where does that power come from? The energy that drives weather comes from the sun.

Earth gets huge amounts of solar (sun) energy. Sunlight pours down on Earth twenty-four hours a day. As Earth spins, half the world is always bathed in sunshine. The sun heats oceans and lakes. It heats the land. Solar energy powers the wind. It creates storms that churn in the atmosphere.

TEMPERATURE DIFFERENCES

What if everything on Earth were exactly the same temperature? There would be no differences in weather! But sunlight doesn't warm everything evenly. It takes a lot of sunlight to raise the temperature of water. Its temperature rises slowly. When the sun shines on land, its temperature rises more quickly. Land cools faster than water too. Water holds the sun's heat longer.

In addition, parts of Earth near the equator get more sunlight than the regions near the North Pole and the South Pole. So some parts of Earth's surface are always warmer than others. Temperatures all over Earth change with the seasons too.

On a sunny, early summer day in Mendocino, California, the air is warm but the water is still too cold for swimming.

HEATING AND COOLING EARTH's SURFACE

Fill a clear plastic cup with soil. Fill another with water. Put a thermometer in each cup. Write down the starting temperatures of both cups.

Put the cups outside in bright sunshine. Check the temperatures every five minutes. Keep recording them. The cup of soil will get warm faster.

After thirty minutes, put the cups in a cool, dark place. Keep checking the temperatures for another thirty minutes. You'll see that the soil cools more quickly too.

In the same way, land heats up faster than lakes and oceans when heated by the sun. It also cools more quickly.

As the sun heats Earth unevenly, it sets the atmosphere in motion. Land that has been warmed quickly heats the air above it. As the air gets warmer, it gets lighter and starts to rise. Large bubbles of warm air rise through the cooler air above. These bubbles are called thermals. Meanwhile, cooler air moves in to take the place of the warm air. This motion in the atmosphere is what we call wind. And it all starts with the sun's energy.

FINDING A THERMAL

You can't see a thermal. But you can see signs of rising air. You may see birds circling in the sky. They are riding thermals. On a sunny day, you may see puffy white cumulus clouds. The clouds form when water vapor carried up by a thermal condenses in the cooler upper air.

THERMALS BUILT THIS FLUFFY CUMULUS CLOUD.

NEW YORK CITY'S TIMES SQUARE IS NEARLY EMPTY DURING A WINTER SNOWSTORM.

SEASONS

In most parts of the world, the atmosphere changes with the seasons. In winter the days are short. The air is cold. Winter storms bring cold, steady rain or snow. In summer the days are long. Temperatures rise. Summer storms are often short and violent. Earth travels around the sun once a year. The seasons change as our planet circles the sun.

As Earth travels, it spins on its axis (an invisible line through the

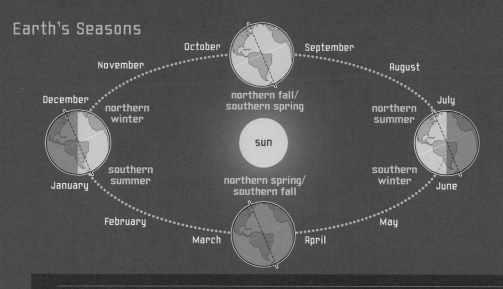

Earth's Seasons

October

September

November

August

December

northern
winter

July

northern
summer

sun

northern fall/
southern spring

southern
summer

January

southern
winter

June

northern spring/
southern fall

February

May

March

April

Earth's angle toward the sun changes as Earth travels through space. This angled movement causes the different seasons.

center from top to bottom). The axis tilts at an angle to the sun. For part of the year, the Northern Hemisphere (northern half of Earth) leans toward the sun. That is summer in the Northern Hemisphere. The days are long. There is more time for the sun to heat Earth. The sun is also high in the sky. So the atmosphere gets warmer.

During the fall months, Earth's tilt toward the sun changes. In winter the Northern Hemisphere tilts away from the sun. It gets less solar energy. The atmosphere gets cooler.

In the Southern Hemisphere, the seasons are reversed. Summer happens during the Northern Hemisphere's winter.

The part of Earth near the equator is never tilted far from the sun. So days and nights are about the same length year-round. The atmosphere stays warm. Places near the equator often have a rainy season and a dry season. But they don't have winter, summer, spring, and fall.

THE ANGLE OF SUNLIGHT

The angle of the sun's rays changes with the seasons. How does this affect the temperature? Try this demonstration. You'll need a sheet of graph paper and a flashlight. Turn off the lights. Shine the flashlight directly down on the paper. Each square gets a lot of light. This direct light is like the sunlight of the summer.

Then keep the flashlight at the same height, but tilt it. Shine it on the paper at an angle. The beam of light spreads out. Each square on the paper gets less light. This weaker light is like the sunlight in winter months, especially far from the equator.

Earth is shaped like a ball. Sunlight is direct and strong near the equator and in the half of Earth tilted toward the sun. At the poles and in the hemisphere tilted away from the sun, sunlight is spread out. It's like light from the tilted flashlight. Even in summer, the light that reaches polar regions is not very strong.

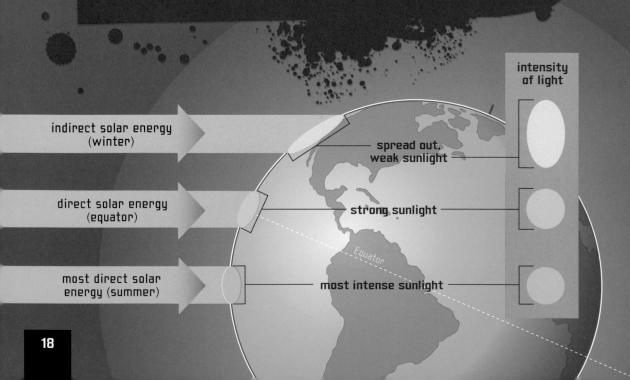

intensity
of light

indirect solar energy
(winter)

spread out,
weak sunlight

direct solar energy
(equator)

strong sunlight

Equator

most direct solar
energy (summer)

most intense sunlight

HEATING AND COOLING WITH ALTITUDE

Air temperature also depends on height in the atmosphere. Air is warmest near Earth's surface. As air rises, its temperature drops about 28°F for each mile (10°C for each kilometer) it climbs.

Cool air holds less water vapor than warm air. So when warm air rises and cools, water vapor condenses (turns from gas into liquid). It forms droplets of liquid water. The droplets create clouds.

Once air has cooled, it sinks lower in the atmosphere. The air gets warmer again.

This up-and-down movement of air is called convection. The winds it produces are called convection currents. These currents, like all weather, are fueled by the heat of the sun.

EARTH'S ENERGY BUDGET

If the sun keeps shining, why doesn't the world keep getting hotter? Some energy is never absorbed by Earth. Earth also loses energy.

Clouds reflect some sunlight back into space. Sunlight bounces off ice and snow-covered land too. Some sunlight bounces off the ocean's surface. Reflected light doesn't heat Earth at all.

Earth also loses heat by radiation (giving off energy). The heat goes back into space. All objects—including Earth—radiate heat. They send out infrared rays. These are a kind of energy. Think of them as heat rays. We can't see infrared rays. But we can feel them.

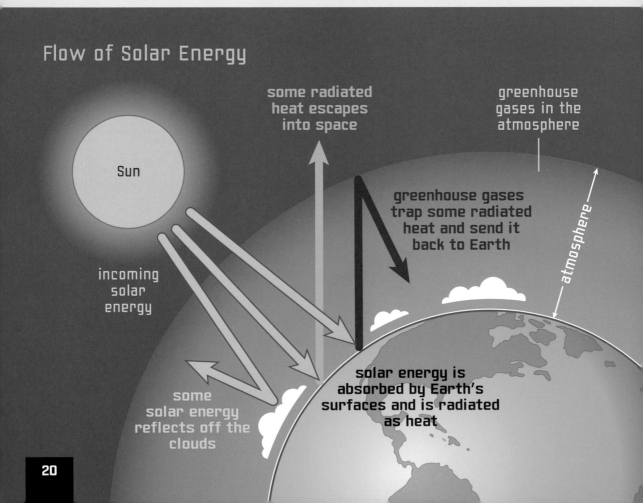

Flow of Solar Energy

Sun

some radiated heat escapes into space

greenhouse gases in the atmosphere

greenhouse gases trap some radiated heat and send it back to Earth

atmosphere

incoming solar energy

some solar energy reflects off the clouds

solar energy is absorbed by Earth's surfaces and is radiated as heat

GREENHOUSE GASES KEEP EARTH WARM ENOUGH FOR LIFE, JUST AS A GREENHOUSE KEEPS PLANTS INSIDE WARM.

The amount of energy flowing to and from our planet is called Earth's energy budget. The world's energy budget is balanced. Earth radiates and reflects almost exactly as much energy as it gets from the sun. That's good for life on Earth. Otherwise, our planet would get too hot or too cold to support life.

Water vapor plays a part in Earth's energy budget. So does carbon dioxide. These gases hold heat in the atmosphere. They act like glass in a greenhouse—they let light and heat in but don't let heat out. Because of this, water vapor and carbon dioxide are called greenhouse gases.

Greenhouse gases are important. Without them, Earth would lose too much heat to space. Earth's average surface temperature is about 59°F (15°C). Without greenhouse gases, the average would be much lower. Earth's temperature would be about 0°F (−18°C). Most plants and animals couldn't survive at that temperature. Our planet would be a lifeless, icy ball.

Water rushes off the edge of a melting glacier in Greenland. Water absorbs more of the sun's rays than ice does. So melting glaciers may speed up Earth's warming.

But greenhouse gases can also cause problems. You probably have heard the term *global warming.* It refers to the recent warming of the world's climates. In the past one hundred years, the average temperature has risen about 1°F (0.6°C). The main cause seems to be more carbon dioxide in the air. The extra carbon dioxide comes from people burning coal, oil, and gas.

Scientists are studying greenhouse gases to find out more about climate change and global warming. They know that keeping Earth's energy budget balanced is important. Weather patterns may change if Earth becomes too warm. Some plants and animals might not survive if climates change too much.

CHAPTER THREE
GLOBAL WIND PATTERNS

The uneven heating of Earth creates areas of high and low pressure. These pressure differences create global wind patterns. The wind patterns move the sun's heat from one part of the atmosphere to another.

The tropics (areas near the equator) get more solar heat than other parts of the world. The warm tropical air is not very dense. It rises and forms an area of low pressure near the equator.

THESE PENGUINS LIVE IN ANTARCTICA, NEAR THE SOUTH POLE. ANTARCTICA IS COLD BECAUSE IT GETS VERY LITTLE SOLAR ENERGY.

Polar regions get much less sun. The cold air there is dense. That dense, cold air creates high pressure at the North Pole and the South Pole.

In general, cold air from the poles moves toward the equator. It takes the place of rising tropical air. The rising air flows back toward the poles. But wind patterns are not quite that simple.

The distance around Earth is much smaller near the poles than near the equator. So the air flowing toward the poles gets squeezed and forced farther upward. The rising air cools as it goes higher. This creates other regions of high pressure.

Bands of high pressure form at about 30° N and S latitude. (Lines of latitude show distance from the equator. The equator is at 0° latitude. The poles are at 90°.) These high pressure zones are called subtropical highs. Here the cool, dense air drops back toward the surface of Earth. Some flows back toward the equator.

This sets up circular patterns of air moving up and down in the atmosphere. These are called Hadley cells. Hadley cells create winds near the surface known as trade winds. These winds blow east to west. Sailors on trading ships once used them to sail west from Europe to the Americas.

Another circular wind pattern forms near the poles. Cold, dense air above the poles sinks and creates a polar high pressure system. The air flows out from the poles toward lower pressure. It produces a wind pattern called a polar cell. Like the trade winds, the polar winds blow from the east. They are called polar easterlies.

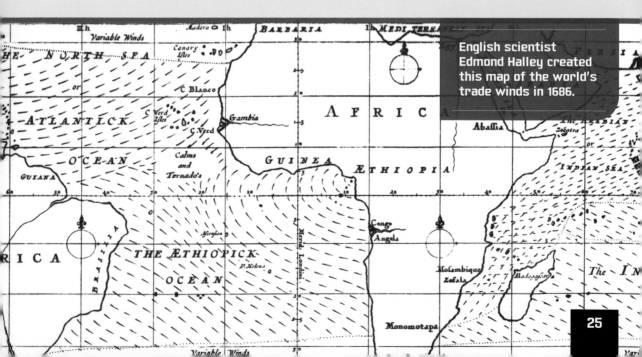

English scientist Edmond Halley created this map of the world's trade winds in 1686.

Polar cells reach from the poles to about 60° N and S latitudes. There, cold air pushes against warmer air from the middle latitudes. The cold polar air warms and rises, and bands of low pressure form. These bands are called subpolar lows.

Air flows from the subtropical highs toward the subpolar lows. This creates a third set of cells. They are called Ferrel cells. Ferrel cells form between about 30° and 60° latitudes in both hemispheres. They produce surface winds that blow from the west, called prevailing westerlies.

Bands of weak, light winds are located between the three cells. One region, called the doldrums, forms near the equator. The word *doldrums* means "a state of boredom or sadness." Sailors in the doldrums could drift for weeks, waiting for a breeze to catch their

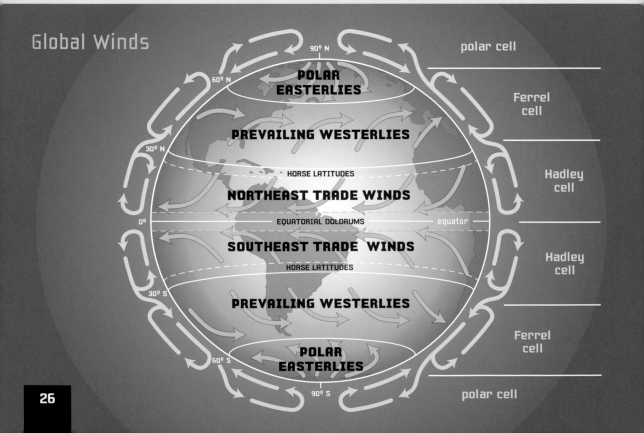

Global Winds

90° N

polar cell

60° N

POLAR EASTERLIES

Ferrel cell

PREVAILING WESTERLIES

30° N

HORSE LATITUDES

Hadley cell

NORTHEAST TRADE WINDS

0°

EQUATORIAL DOLDRUMS

equator

SOUTHEAST TRADE WINDS

Hadley cell

HORSE LATITUDES

30° S

PREVAILING WESTERLIES

Ferrel cell

POLAR EASTERLIES

60° S

90° S

polar cell

Few clouds cover the ocean west of South America in the horse latitudes.

sails. Around 30° N and S are other areas of weak wind. Sailors called these regions horse latitudes. Sailors might wait so long for a breeze that they'd have to eat their horses for food or throw them overboard to save resources.

JET STREAMS

Flowing air also creates winds at the top of the troposphere. These fast-moving rivers of air are called jet streams. Polar and subtropical jet streams circle the globe in both the Northern Hemisphere and the Southern Hemisphere.

FASCINATING FACT:

Hadley cells are named for British scientist George Hadley. He first described them in 1753. Ferrel cells are named for William Ferrel, a U.S. meteorologist. He described them in 1856.

The jet streams form where warmer air meets cool polar air. Jet streams are strongest in the winter months. These powerful winds sometimes blow at 200 miles (320 km) per hour.

People discovered jet streams in the 1940s. Pilots of high-flying aircraft discovered they could ride these air currents. The winds let them fly faster and use less fuel. But when they flew in the opposite direction, the wind slowed them down. They learned to fly lower, below the jet stream, in these cases.

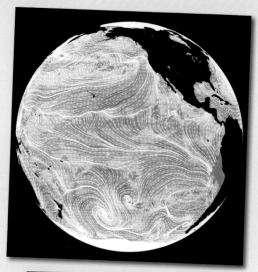

THIS SATELLITE IMAGE SHOWS GLOBAL WIND PATTERNS.

Weather forecasters carefully track where jet streams are blowing. These currents help them make predictions. Jet streams guide the paths of high and low pressure systems. Low pressure systems bring storms. High pressure systems bring clear weather, with cooler, drier air.

THE CORIOLIS EFFECT

Earth rotates from west to east. The rotation has an interesting effect on winds and ocean currents. They bend to the right of their original direction in the Northern Hemisphere. In the Southern Hemisphere, they bend to the left of their original direction. Gaspard-Gustave de

Coriolis described this effect in 1835. It is called the Coriolis effect. Here's how it works.

Everything on Earth's surface is moving east. But a point on Earth near the equator moves much faster than a spot near the poles. It covers more distance in the same amount of time. As a result, objects moving from one point on Earth to another are turned.

Imagine a rocket traveling from the North Pole toward the equator. The rocket flies in a straight line heading south. But Earth is turning eastward beneath it. The surface moves by at a faster and faster rate. To a viewer on Earth, the rocket would seem to turn right—in this case, toward the west.

All moving objects experience the Coriolis effect, including air. And it works for objects traveling in any direction. The faster an object moves, the stronger the effect. The Coriolis effect is strongest at the poles. It disappears at the equator.

In the Northern Hemisphere, the Coriolis effect turns high pressure systems in a clockwise direction. It makes winds spin counterclockwise around stormy low pressure systems. The faster the wind blows, the more the Coriolis effect turns it. This helps create the tight spiral of a powerful hurricane.

The Coriolis Effect

North Pole

intended path

actual path

actual target

equator

intended target

Earth's eastward rotation

amount path is bent by the Coriolis effect

THE CORIOLIS EFFECT BENDS THE PATH OF AN OBJECT FLYING SOUTH FROM THE NORTH POLE. THE OBJECT WOULD CURVE TO THE WEST AND MISS ITS INTENDED TARGET.

South of the equator, the Coriolis effect turns wind in the opposite directions. Low pressure systems spin clockwise. And high pressure systems spin counterclockwise.

Landmasses also affect the direction of wind. Wind blows across the land. The land slows the wind. Have you ever noticed low and high clouds moving in different directions on a windy day? That's usually because low-level winds blow more slowly. The slower winds aren't turned as much by the Coriolis effect.

THE CORIOLIS EFFECT

You can demonstrate the Coriolis effect on your own with a globe of the world and a washable marker. Put the globe on a table. Place your marker at the North Pole. Have a helper turn the globe to the east. While the globe turns, draw a line straight down toward the South Pole. Use the frame that supports the globe to guide the marker's path.

You drew a perfectly straight line. But you'll see that its path curves. It forms the shape of an S. The line bends clockwise in the Northern Hemisphere. The line curves counterclockwise in the Southern Hemisphere.

CHAPTER FOUR

WATER IN THE ATMOSPHERE

Water vapor is an important part of the air. Water vapor is the gas form of water. Like air, water vapor is clear and colorless. The amount of water vapor in the air is always changing. The warmer the air, the more water vapor it can hold. Humidity is the measure of how much water vapor is in the air. When a lot of water vapor is in the air, we say the air is humid. Air can be as much as 4 percent water vapor on hot days. On cold, clear days, water vapor makes up less than 1 percent of the air.

SOIL DRIES OUT AND CRACKS
APART AS THE
SUN'S HEAT CAUSES
WATER TO EVAPORATE.

EVAPORATION AND CONDENSATION

Water enters the air by evaporating, or changing from liquid to gas. Most water vapor in the air evaporates from the oceans. But water also evaporates from land. Summer heat dries out the soil. Trees and plants also take in a lot of water from the soil. Then water evaporates from their leaves.

Evaporation takes a lot of energy. Molecules of liquid water need extra energy to become gas. The energy doesn't change the water's temperature. It just changes its state.

Water molecules carry that extra energy with them into the atmosphere. In this way, water vapor plays a big role in creating Earth's weather. It moves huge amounts of energy around the atmosphere. Water vapor travels with the wind. The molecules carry their heat with them.

When water vapor cools, it condenses, or changes from gas to liquid. It forms tiny water droplets. The droplets become clouds. The clouds release the water in the form of rain or snow. The water leaves the atmosphere and returns to Earth's surface.

SOME OF THE WATER IN
THIS BOTTLE HAS EVAPORATED
AND THEN CONDENSED INTO
DROPLETS AT THE TOP OF
THE BOTTLE.

Dew forms on the ground and other surfaces as they cool overnight. Water vapor from the air condenses to form droplets on the surface.

When water vapor condenses, it releases the energy stored in it. This energy warms the surrounding air. The warm air rises higher. This provides energy to fuel storms such as thunderstorms and hurricanes.

CLOUDS

Clouds are groups of tiny water droplets or ice crystals. The droplets condense on dust or other particles in the air. Clouds come in many different types. The type depends on where in the atmosphere a cloud forms. Meteorologists divide clouds into four main groups. These are high clouds, middle clouds, low clouds, and clouds with vertical (up-and-down) growth.

Wispy cirrus clouds are high clouds. They are made of ice crystals. Middle clouds include flat, gray altostratus clouds.

FASCINATING FACT:

Matter comes in three states—solid, liquid, and gas. Water is a very unusual substance. It's found on Earth in all three states (ice, water, and water vapor).

They cover the sky like a sheet. Altocumulus clouds are middle clouds that look like rows of puffy, gray cotton balls. Low clouds include gray stratus clouds. They often bring fog or drizzle. Nimbostratus clouds are another type of low cloud. They bring steady rain.

Cumulus clouds have vertical growth. They are fair-weather clouds. They form when water vapor rises into cooler air on a thermal. Cumulonimbus clouds have vertical growth too. They are also called thunderheads. They create violent rainstorms with gusty wind and lightning.

MOUNTAINS AND MOISTURE

Land formations affect humidity, rain, and snow. When winds blow across mountain ranges, the moving air rises above the mountains. It gets cooler. Moisture in the air condenses into clouds and falls on the

The Great Smoky Mountains are along the border of Tennessee and North Carolina. They get their name from the clouds and fog that usually cover their slopes. The clouds form when warm, humid air from the Gulf of Mexico blows over the mountains and cools off.

mountains as rain or snow. On the far side of the mountains, the air is much drier. The dry area beyond the mountains is called a rain shadow. The land below gets very little rain.

In the southwestern United States, damp winds blow from the Pacific Ocean. The air rises over the peaks of the Sierra Nevadas. Water vapor condenses. The western side of the mountains gets plenty of rain and snow. But east of the mountains, the air has been squeezed dry. The Mojave Desert and Death Valley are here. They are the driest places in North America.

OCEANS AFFECT EARTH'S WEATHER

Oceans cover about 70 percent of Earth. They have a large effect on the atmosphere. The oceans absorb a huge amount of solar heat. The heat in warm ocean waters provides the energy for tropical storms and hurricanes.

HURRICANE NORBERT FORMED OFF THE COAST OF MEXICO IN 2008.

Water warms and cools slowly. In summer ocean water is usually cooler than nearby land. Ocean water cools the air above it. In winter the ocean is usually warmer than the land. The air above stays warm.

So winters near the coast are milder than they are inland. And coastal summers are usually cooler.

Ocean currents move heat from the tropics to cooler regions. Global wind patterns help create the currents. Wind blows across the ocean surface day after day. The wind pushes the surface waters along with it. This creates currents in the ocean.

The Gulf Stream is a current along the Atlantic coast of North America. This current carries warm tropical Atlantic water up the coast. It warms the air and land. It even carries heat across the Atlantic to Europe.

Cold ocean currents carry northern water back to the tropics. The cold California Current is part of the Pacific Ocean. It flows south along the west coast of North America. When the air inland is sweltering, this current keeps the coastal lands cool.

IN THIS SATELLITE IMAGE, THE WARMEST WATERS OF THE GULF STREAM OFF THE COAST OF NORTH CAROLINA APPEAR IN PINK. COOLER WATER IS SHOWN IN PURPLE AND BLUE.

CHAPTER FIVE

THE EVER-CHANGING ATMOSPHERE

One thing about the weather is certain. It never stops changing. The atmosphere is always in motion. Winds blow from one part of Earth to another. The wind moves solar energy with it. Storms travel with the winds. So do areas of fair weather. Local conditions also have an effect on weather.

SEMIPERMANENT HIGHS AND LOWS

Even though the weather is always changing, many weather patterns repeat year after year. For example, regions of high and low pressure form in the same areas each year. The uneven heating of land and oceans creates these large areas of high and low pressure.

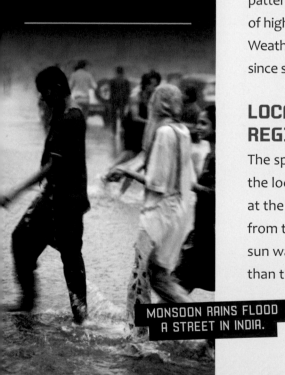

MONSOON RAINS FLOOD A STREET IN INDIA.

In summer a high pressure system is usually over the cool North Atlantic Ocean. Meteorologists call this the Bermuda High. A Pacific high forms off the coast of Alaska and Canada. Meanwhile, the air over the land is warmer. Low pressure forms there.

In winter the pattern reverses. High pressure forms over the cooler land. Lows form over the warmer oceans.

These weather patterns are semipermanent because they change with the seasons. The patterns create winds as air blows from areas of high pressure to areas of low pressure. Weather patterns also affect storm patterns, since storms form in regions of low pressure.

LOCAL AND REGIONAL WEATHER

The special conditions of each place affect the local weather. For example, weather at the top of a mountain is very different from the weather in the nearby valley. The sun warms the sides of a mountain faster than the valley. As the mountainside warms during the day, the air above it rises. A warm wind often blows up from the valley. Clouds form

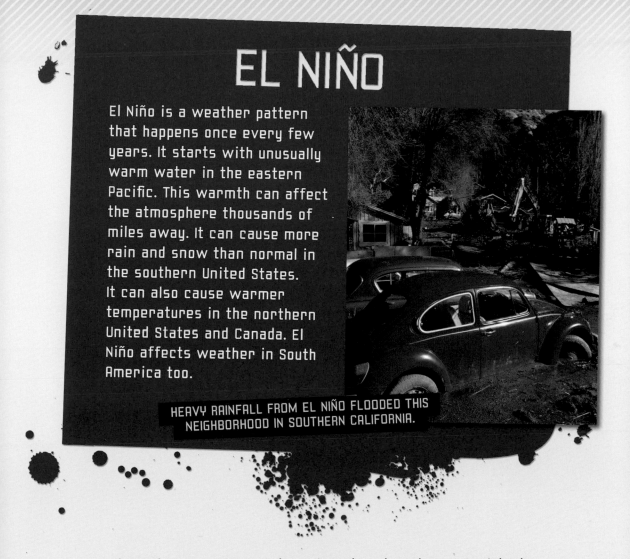

EL NIÑO

El Niño is a weather pattern that happens once every few years. It starts with unusually warm water in the eastern Pacific. This warmth can affect the atmosphere thousands of miles away. It can cause more rain and snow than normal in the southern United States. It can also cause warmer temperatures in the northern United States and Canada. El Niño affects weather in South America too.

HEAVY RAINFALL FROM EL NIÑO FLOODED THIS NEIGHBORHOOD IN SOUTHERN CALIFORNIA.

above the mountaintops where air cools and condenses. At night the mountaintops cool quickly. Cool breezes blow down into the valley.

Seashores have a similar wind pattern. During the day, the land heats quickly. The warm air above it rises. Cooler ocean air rushes in to take its place. The pattern reverses at night. The land cools. The ocean is warmer. Breezes blow from the land toward the ocean.

Another local weather pattern occurs near the Great Lakes in North America. In early winter, winds blow across the lakes from the west. The wind picks up water vapor as it moves over the warmer water. Then it blows across the colder land. The vapor condenses and falls as snow south and east of the lakes. This snowfall is called lake-effect snow.

DOWNSLOPE WINDS

Sometimes winds push across a mountain range and into a valley below. As the air drops, its pressure increases. The air gets warmer.

These downslope (downward) winds are common in Southern California. Hot, dry winds push down the mountains toward the coast. Californians call them Santa Ana winds.

Other parts of the world also have downslope winds. In the eastern Rocky Mountains, they are called Chinook winds or "snow eaters" because they melt the snow. Around the Mediterranean Sea, they are called the sirocco.

THE HOT, DRY SANTA ANA WINDS SPREAD WILDFIRES IN CALIFORNIA IN NOVEMBER 2008.

HUMAN ACTIVITY

People affect the atmosphere too. We do this partly by building cities. Stone and brick buildings hold heat. We also heat buildings during the winter. In this way, cities become "heat islands." Air in the city is often warmer than in the nearby countryside. This difference in temperature creates local breezes. Tall buildings also heat up during the day and cool at night, creating smaller local breezes much like a mountain does.

Cutting trees to make space for homes or farms also affects the atmosphere. Trees serve as windbreaks. Their roots hold the soil in place. They provide cooling shade. Fallen leaves hold moisture in the soil, where it can later evaporate. When people clear forests, a region can become hotter and drier. It can even turn into a desert.

WHEN LOGGERS CUT DOWN MOST OF THE TREES IN AN AREA, IT IS KNOWN AS CLEAR-CUTTING.

Aircraft exhaust scatters tiny particles into the air. Water vapor condenses on the particles. This can form long, thin clouds called contrails. These human-made clouds sometimes spread across the sky behind a plane. Fires, whether natural or human-made, also put particles into the air. Water condenses on these particles too.

HEAVY TRAFFIC FILLS A HIGHWAY IN LOS ANGELES, CALIFORNIA. CARS RELEASE CARBON DIOXIDE AND OTHER POLLUTION INTO THE ATMOSPHERE.

Burning fuel to power cars, create electricity, and heat buildings releases carbon dioxide. Carbon dioxide is a greenhouse gas. It becomes part of the atmosphere and traps heat near Earth. In recent centuries, humans have used more and more carbon-based fuel, adding more carbon dioxide to the atmosphere. People have also cleared forests. So there are fewer trees to remove carbon dioxide from the air. Most scientists think the extra carbon dioxide is slowly raising Earth's temperature. They think temperatures will continue to rise in the future.

Some scientists think Earth's temperature will rise by about 3 to 7°F (1.8 to 4°C) by the end of the twenty-first century. If we limit the amount of carbon-based fuel we use, the change could be less. But no one knows just how much warmer Earth may get or how rising temperatures may affect life on our planet. Earth's atmosphere is complicated. Predicting what will happen to the atmosphere over many years is very difficult.

PREDICTING THE WEATHER

Everything that happens in the atmosphere affects the weather. And the weather in one place may be affected by events thousands of miles away. This makes weather forecasting tricky.

Meteorologists use computers to gather information about weather patterns across the United States. Their findings become the weather reports given on television, in the newspaper, and on the Internet.

Meteorologists take measurements at thousands of weather stations. Satellites also circle Earth in space. These machines help gather more data from the atmosphere than ever before. Scientists study all this information with powerful computers. But it's impossible to measure everything. So no one can predict the weather perfectly. But the more we know about the atmosphere, the better we can understand its patterns and forecast the weather.

GLOSSARY

aerosols: tiny particles that float in the air

air pressure: the force of air pushing down on Earth

atmosphere: the blanket of gases that surrounds Earth's surface

barometer: an instrument that measures air pressure

climate: average weather conditions of a place over many years

condense: to change from a gas to a liquid

Coriolis effect: an effect of Earth's rotation that causes the path of any moving object to bend

doldrums: a region near Earth's equator with low air pressure and weak winds

evaporate: to change from a liquid to a gas

Ferrel cells: midlatitude (about 30° to 60° N and S) regions of the atmosphere where winds circle the globe in regular patterns

front: the zone where two different air masses meet

global warming: the recent warming of Earth's surface and the air just above it; a condition probably caused by increased carbon dioxide and other heat-trapping gases in the atmosphere

gravity: a force that pulls objects toward one another

greenhouse gases: gases, including water vapor and carbon dioxide, that hold heat in the atmosphere

Hadley cells: regions of the atmosphere on either side of the equator where winds circle the globe in regular patterns

horse latitudes: warm, dry regions of Earth near 30° N and S latitude with high air pressure and weak winds

jet streams: narrow bands of fast-moving wind at the top of the troposphere

mesosphere: the layer of the atmosphere between the stratosphere and the thermosphere, about 30 to 50 miles (50 to 80 km) above Earth's surface

meteorology: the science of weather

monsoon: a pattern of wet and dry winds in Asia that reverse direction with the seasons

polar easterlies: surface winds that blow from the east near both the North Pole and the South Pole

prevailing westerlies: surface winds that blow from the west in the middle latitudes of both the Northern Hemisphere and the Southern Hemisphere

rain shadow: an area downwind of a mountain range that gets little rain because the clouds have released their moisture over the mountains

stratosphere: a stable layer of the atmosphere above the troposphere, about 6.6 to 30 miles (11 to 50 km) above Earth's surface

thermal: a large bubble of warm air that rises up through the atmosphere

thermosphere: the uppermost layer of the atmosphere, more than 50 miles (80 km) above Earth's surface

trade winds: surface winds that blow from the east on either side of the equator

troposphere: the lowest level of the atmosphere, up to about 6.6 miles (11 km) above Earth's surface, where all weather takes place

weather: the current condition of the atmosphere in a certain place

SELECTED BIBLIOGRAPHY

Aguardo, Edward, and James E. Burt. *Understanding Weather & Climate.* 3rd ed. Upper Saddle River, NJ: Prentice Hall, 2004.

Ahrens, C. Donald. *Meteorology Today.* 8th ed. Belmont, CA: Thompson Higher Education, 2007.

Allaby, Michael. *The Facts on File Weather and Climate Handbook.* New York: Facts on File, 2002.

Lutgens, Frederick, and Edward J. Tarbuck. *The Atmosphere: An Introduction to Meteorology.* 10th ed. Upper Saddle River, NJ: Prentice Hall, 2006.

Mayes, Julian. *Understanding Weather: A Visual Approach.* London: Arnold, 2004.

Reynolds, Ross. *Firefly Guide to Weather.* Buffalo: Firefly Books, 2005.

FURTHER READING

Carson, Mary Kay. *Weather Projects for Young Scientists: Experiments and Science Fair Ideas.* Chicago: Chicago Review Press, 2007. The activities in this book let students see atmospheric concepts at work, build a barometer, make frost, trap air pollution particles, and much more.

Fleisher, Paul. *Vapor, Rain, and Snow: The Science of Clouds and Precipitation.* Minneapolis: Lerner, 2011. This book in the Weatherwise series explores how water in the atmosphere forms clouds, drizzle, hail, and more. Also check out *Lightning, Hurricanes, and Blizzards* and *Doppler Radar, Satellites, and Computer Models* to explore storms and weather forecasting.

Gallant, Roy A. *Atmosphere: Sea of Air.* New York: Benchmark Books, 2003. With diagrams and photos, this text explores the atmosphere as well as storms, rainbows, and global warming.

Johnson, Rebecca L. *Understanding Global Warming.* Minneapolis: Lerner Publications Company, 2009. Learn more about Earth's rising temperature, why human actions are most likely the cause, and how we can tackle this global problem.

Rapp, Valerie. *Protecting Earth's Air Quality.* Minneapolis: Lerner Publications Company, 2009. From driving cars to turning on lights, things that people do every day pollute the atmosphere. Find out how we affect Earth's air and what we can do to protect it.

Woodward, John. *Weather.* London: DK Pub., 2007. This book in the DK e.guides series explores weather around the world through straightforward text and vivid graphics. A companion website offers further exploration.

WEBSITES

United States National Weather Service
http://www.nws.noaa.gov/
Visit this site to explore weather maps, get forecasts, learn about climates and weather safety, and even sign up for text messages from the U.S. National Weather Service.

The Weather Channel Kids
http://www.theweatherchannelkids.com/
Check out the Weather Channel's site for students to find forecasts, use a weather encyclopedia, read about weather safety for your pets, and more.

Weather Research
http://www.research.noaa.gov/weather/
Find out how the U.S. National Oceanic and Atmospheric Administration is studying the atmosphere and different types of weather with weather balloons, radar, satellites, and other high-tech and low-tech tools.

Web Weather for Kids
http://www.eo.ucar.edu/webweather/
This site includes hands-on weather experiments and activities. You can also read true-life stories of wild weather, and try your hand at making a forecast.

INDEX

ABOUT THE AUTHOR

Paul Fleisher is a veteran educator and the author of dozens of science titles for children, including the Secrets of the Universe series, the Early Bird Food Web series, and *The Big Bang* and *Evolution* for the Great Ideas of Science series. He is also the author of *Parasites: Latching On to a Free Lunch.* He lives with his wife in Richmond, Virginia.

PHOTO ACKNOWLEDGMENTS

The images in this book are used with the permission of: © Artman/Dreamstime.com, p. 1; © SuperStock/SuperStock, pp. 3, 5 (top); © Dennis MacDonald/Alamy, p. 4; © Photodisc/ Getty Images, p. 5 (bottom); © Pete Turner/Stone/Getty Images, p. 6; © Joel Sartore/ National Geographic/Getty Images, p. 7; © Laura Westlund/Independent Picture Service, pp. 8, 17, 18, 20, 26, 29; © Bill Stevenson/Aurora/Getty Images, p. 9; © Stefan Zaklin/Getty Images, p. 10; © Svlumagraphica/Dreamstime.com, p. 12; © Chris Holland/Photonica/Getty Images, p. 13; © George Rose/Getty Images, p. 14; © 2ndpic/Dreamstime.com, p. 16 (top); © age fotostock/SuperStock, pp. 16 (bottom), 38; © Ben Heys/Dreamstime.com, p. 19; © Hudakore/Dreamstime.com, p. 21; © James Balog/Aurora/Getty Images, p. 22; © Robert Harding Picture Library/SuperStock, p. 23; © David Tipling/Photographer's Choice/Getty Images, p. 24; NASA/JPL, p. 25 (top); © Royal Astronomical Society/Photo Researchers, Inc., p. 25 (bottom); © Stocktrek Images/Getty Images, p. 27; © Science Source/Photo Researchers, Inc., p. 28; © Jonathan Vasata/Dreamstime.com, p. 30; © iStockphoto.com/ Björn Kindler, p. 31; © Lilia Barladyan/Dreamstime.com, p. 32 (top); © Jeecis/Dreamstime. com, p. 32 (bottom); © Dmytro Tokar/Dreamstime.com, p. 33; © Tony Sweet/Digital Vision/ Getty Images, p. 34; © Stocktrek RF/Getty Images, p. 35; NASA, p. 36; © Jason Edwards/ National Geographic/Getty Images, p. 37; © Todd Bigelow/Aurora/Getty Images, p. 39; © David McNew/Getty Images, p. 40; © Thinkstock/Comstock Images/Getty Images, p. 41; AP Photo/Damian Dovarganes, p. 42; © Kim Steele/Photodisc/Getty Images, p. 43.

Front Cover: © Diane Cook and Len Jenshel/Stone/Getty Images.
Back Cover: © iStockphoto.com/Nadezda Firsova.